To those who thought I could,
those who knew I would,
and to those who said I couldn't.

I Dream in Color

It's a story about a girl
whose dreams were so far away,
that she began her journey entangled in an impossible
straightjacket of twisted seaweed,
chaining her to the depths of the darkness,
thousands of feet under the deep black sea,
surrounded by sharks who wanted to eat her for
breakfast, lunch, and dinner,
where she relished in, the very least, her ability to dream
of one day not just escaping,
but of shining like a star in the sky,
and upon finally freeing herself after chewing away at the
seaweed that tasted of horrid, rancid, muck for years,
set out to craft a makeshift submarine
from thousand-year-old sunken treasure
and garbage that others had tossed away,
to which she entered said submarine and rose to the surface
over many, many days,
surviving on a measly diet of cold fish stew,
which was still superior culinary fare to the seaweed,
only then to be greeted by turbulent seas in which she,
all the while being pushed around by the waves
and nearly drowned,
swallowing copious amounts of sickening sea water,
and gasping for air at every receding wave,
managed to disassemble the submarine to fashion a sailboat,
so that she could navigate the rough waters from above
to the only island around for miles and miles,
all the while admiring the stars in the sky,

and selecting her special one,
where after a bit of time she finally docked,
after having lost her already tattered and pathetic sail
in a terrible gust of wind,
leaving her to paddle with her arms,
one of them broken,
the final five miles,
to find just enough food and fresh water
to last but a few months,
and just enough shells and pearls
to make a collection of tokens she could wear around her neck
for the remainder of her journey,
and just enough beached wreckage and ancient learning text
to where she could build a personal flying machine
to get her off of the island
and on to the top of the highest mountain,
and even though her belly was full and she achieved
a certain amount of contentment on the not-so-tropical island,
she knew she still had so far to go,
and sadly couldn't remain,
but before she was entirely ready,
was forced to evacuate by a hurricane and great storm,
that produced a fierce lightning strike,
which caused a fire so hot and so ravenous,
that all of the animal friends followed her,
in what would now be deemed as the most beautiful
hot-air balloon any of them had ever laid eyes on,
that she had been building as a thing merely of beauty,
simply out of enjoyment to pass the time while she waited,
not knowing of its true capabilities
or intentions of being a vehicle to her destiny,

until the moment it dawned on her
that the fire that was set out to destroy her
was now the most useful tool at her disposal,
lifting, by its heat,
the great balloon into the sky,
where some animals escaped inside the basket with her
just in time,
others in which, by the grace of creation,
had wings of their own by nature,
and so were able to fly alongside,
and on their way up,
they waved goodbye to those who were too heavy
for the delicate and beautifully weaved basket,
and some that just didn't believe
that the basket would hold,
and things were good,
but after flying for weeks and weeks,
the harsh winds that once aided them
eventually wore away at the weakest seam
and exposed it,
where a crash landing was made,
more goodbyes were said,
and she took to the skies once again
on the wings of a magnificent eagle,
who assisted her in catching and eating bugs and leaves
while soaring through the air,
and drinking the mist and rain droplets from the clouds,
to which the time finally came that
the eagle led her to the mountain top,
where they landed in dense forest,
rich in commodities, danger, and uncertainty,

where she was able to excavate
just enough precious metals
from the land's available resources
that she could use to then engineer a spacecraft
to pilot herself to the first star in the sky,
which she had been eyeing for some time now,
which was also marked on her very worn, very tired, map,
where upon her way,
her very long way,
she was faced with a fire-breathing dragon,
of the not-so-friendly variety,
whose breath of fire engulfed her treasured map
like it was nothing,
dissolving it into but a few specs of ash
that escaped the tips of her fingers and blew away,
to which she promptly rectified
with a swift death sentence of the dragon
issued by the tip of her sword,
and upon emerging from the throes of the vicious duel,
removed the dragon's claw as a keepsake,
and added it to her special token necklace,
then took refuge in the safety of the spacecraft,
where, realizing she was out of fuel,
cried for a few days at first,
but then put good use to her crocodile tears
by adding them to the fuel tank,
which sputtered, whined, and complained,
but ultimately, slowly, but surely,
got her there,
where upon that star she met with other
fellow dreamers, who told of their journeys thus far,

and shared in her first hot meal in years,
and it was so good,
and after a few days of harrowing stories
around the crackling fire
they each abandoned the safety of their spaceships,
and swam peacefully through the sea of stars,
some making their way in opposite directions,
without regard for bed times or dinner times,
where she and a few others headed straight to the moon
upon where she planted the seeds
she had collected along the way in her pocket,
in hopes of one day growing a garden of trees,
not knowing if her efforts would be met
with just the right amount of rain,
and just the right amount of sun,
but to her delight they were,
by pure grace,
and over many, many years of waiting and tending,
and waiting,
and tending,
and waiting,
and tending,
the once desolate surface of the moon
was now overflowing with
crystal clear waterfalls, voluminous greenery, exotic plants,
flowers of all varieties, endless bounties of fruit,
crickety bridges leading from tree to tree,
twisted swings of vines adorned with all the colors of the rainbow,
birds with hats,
birds without hats,
fantastical treehouses,
magical creatures,

and all sorts of surprise things
she hadn't even dreamed of,
or even planted to begin with,
where now all could partake and enjoy,
without once looking back,
except to see how far away
and how small the Earth's ocean truly was
from that ultimate peak,
reveling at how,
at one time in history,
long, long ago,
it had swallowed her whole and surrounded her
like the mouth of a giant whale,
and then,
for a very long second,
she smiled,
knowing that what she had done was good,
and that she had, in fact,
made it.

every

Journey begins with one step

-Lao Tzu

Just when the Caterpillar ~thought her world was over~ She became a Butterfly

- English Proverb

All the flowers of tomorrow are in the seeds of today

-Indian Proverb

Who is this girl? Who is this unstoppable,
beautifully broken, courageous girl who can slay
dragons, swim for miles with a broken arm,
overcome any obstacle in her path,
build something out of nothing...
and then fly it to the stars in the sky?

"She's you."

Today
was
amazing because...

A Message from Hannah

Hi everyone! Thank you so much for purchasing a copy of my book. This is my personal story of how I started from nothing to get to where I am today; but it's also your story, and your friend's story, and so many others' stories! We all face challenges in life, and drawing and coloring has always been a saving grace for me, ever since I was a young child. I welcomed art back into my life and started "adult coloring" in 2006 as a stay at home mom and full time online business student as a way to manage the daily stresses of life, and also as a way to escape the physical pain from very serious autoimmune arthritis that has been with me since I was 11 years old. I started with a pack of kid's quality colored pencils and cardstock from the local drugstore market, and got back to drawing again. Since we didn't have a lot of money while trying to raise a young family, I had to find a way to at least cover the costs of my new hobby, so I did some research and put some of my artwork up for auction online. I have since sold thousands of paintings, sketches, prints, products, and coloring books. There have been no agents, no editors, no publishers, no marketing teams, no cover designers, no investors, and no formal educators. This book is a labor of love and mine from start to finish! It is the realization of many, many years of hard work, tears, failures, physical pain, broken dreams, and mental strain. It has also been the most amazing journey I've ever been on, and I wouldn't trade it for anything in the world.

My story continues, and so will yours. I still fail. That's part of reaching out beyond what you know is guaranteed; if you're not failing, you're not really stretching outside of your comfort zone. I decided I would much prefer to risk being disappointed once in a while in exchange for having the satisfied feeling of really succeeding, and I'm here to tell you I'm really glad I did. There are few things better in life than setting a goal just outside of your reach, working hard, and then achieving it. When faced with the difficult path or the easy path, choose the difficult path; it will lead you to places that you never dreamed were possible. Make a wish, and then make it happen! With my drawing hand suffering from permanent joint damage and subsequently a limited range of mobility from years of living with arthritis, it's hard to believe I can even draw with it, but I have been for years! I refuse to allow anything to limit my potential. The only limitations you have are those that you set for yourself. Treat yourself well and rest when you need to, but don't ever give up.

We all know that we can't make it in this world truly alone. I would like to thank you, my fans, for supporting me, God for being my constant source of strength when I had nothing left to give, and my husband of 18 years for being by my side through every step in a very real, very supportive way. Without these things, I wouldn't be where I am today and I am so very grateful!

I hope you enjoy this book and that it inspires you to reach out for something you've been dreaming about, or gives you renewed strength to continue on your journey!

Happy Coloring & Dreaming!

Hannah

Printed in Great Britain
by Amazon